Emotional Truth

Lily Graham

Presentation by *BookLeaf Publishing*

Web: www.bookleafpub.com

E-mail: info@bookleafpub.com

ISBN: 978-93-95784-91-7

First edition 2022

ACKNOWLEDGEMENT

Always was, Always will be.

PREFACE

Secrets are things we keep inside, while stories are things we let out. Emotions are something I held in for a long time and here I let them out through story.

Vulnerable

I'm scared
Cannot be repaired
So weak
Cannot speak

Weak is what I've been declared
I need to be more prepared
Need to try a new technique
Knowing It will face critique

Sick of being compared
Due for the worst but I've been spared
Needing more than I can seek
Everything is looking bleak

Hope

Stomping round, see me mope
My life is but a slippery slope
Pretending like I don't care
But really here in disrepair

Living life through horoscope
The only thing that gives me hope
Enough of all the wear and tear
I know now, I am aware

Learning new ways to cope
Maybe I do have scope
Feeling that the hope is there
Finally feel the flow of air

Anxiety

I want to go, but know I can't attend
I feel alone, not even one friend
Part of me knows that's just not the case
The other part demands I can't show my face

It's much easier to hide and pretend
Known as the one who you cannot depend
I feel my heart race
My breath, I seek to chase

The feeling I have, I don't think will mend
I'm sure in this moment, this is my end
Stuck on this earth- it's just not my place
Anxiety tells me I am a freak from space.

Aspiration

Looking around, no one to admire
Everyone does what they each desire
I am told I'll be just like them
My purpose In life to cause mayhem

I will show them that makes them a liar
It's time now for that narrative to retire
I may come from that stem
And I may not be pretty or femme

But Inside me I have a wild raging fire
All I can do is try hard and aspire
I know with hard work I can be a gem
I will leave not a thing for you to condemn

Angry

So angry, I'm full of rage
It puts so many in a cage
Acting without the thought of backlash
Then realise we have to dash

Behaviour won't differ no matter my age
Looking at the world like it is my stage
I won't be made out to be brash
All we do together is argue and clash

I need to turn a different page
Leave at once and not engage
You infest my mind just like a rash
But I still refuse to bang or bash!

Proud

I vowed
To always be loud
No regret for taking this route
These are my morals and what I'm about

I am proud
Alone or in a crowd
I'll be there to shout
Without a doubt

Even when it's not allowed
Everyone knows she is avowed
Regardless of clout
I will always call it out

Fear

I cannot forget the sound in my ear
That noise instantly triggers my fear
When the wrath comes all we can do is hide
I can't stop it, boy have I tried

Soon realising this is only first gear
Now it won't stop, tear after tear
Once again you have lied
Here we are, no one to confide

This is just part of your career
Getting away with it year after year
It's not personal taking us along for the ride
So impersonal, couldn't care if we died.

Appreciation

know that it's fate
That I was there on that date
It may have been subtle
But I couldn't be more greatful

Maybe it happened late
But I know it was worth the wait
I was starting to be doubtful
Thinking I would stumble

Now I see straight
So thankful my life is great
Experiences fruitful
Always keeping humble

Shame

I'm just a child
They've all gone wild
There is a claim
And I'm not not blame

I'm sure this is mild
But now it's all filed
Sitting here feeling so shame
Wait for the people to load and take aim

I know that it's piled
So once more they're dialled
Sometimes I wonder if life is a game
I often wonder will I be the same?

Faith

As I sit here and plead
I watch my life bleed
Caught in the grip
Sinking like a ship

It is faith that I need
I want to succeed
Yet see myself slip
This time I can't skip

I need to exceed
I know I'll be freed
Crack of a whip
Cut all ties with a snip

Guilt

Why did I leave?
Because I can't sit and watch you all theive
We were stitched together like a quilt
But I'm seeing my life turn on a tilt

I cannot deceive
I just want to be better and achieve
I'm strong because that's how Ive been built
However I am filled with guilt

For I always wear my heart on my sleeve
I cannot believe
Watching all the effort spilt
Watching myself fade like a flower does wilt

Excitement

No one knew
What we would accrue
Completely unsighted
Im so excited

And this that we grew
Here through and through
Together united
Something ignited

Now they get in a queue
To see how we flew
Achievements highlighted
So pleased and delighted

Grief

Here I lay drowning in the rain
How could I ever bear this pain
I never knew this day was nigh
And now we will never know why

The grief holds me down like a chain
You never wish to know this strain
We see you when we look to the Sky
There you have your wings to fly

I feel myself going insane
I know my heart can't cope again
Although eventually we all die
So for now we had to say goodbye

Happiness

Happy or content
It's a rare event
More than I could visualise
Riding all the highs

Like the peak of a tent
In sight, no decent
Can't believe my eyes
Here I am on the rise

Sturdy like cement
Can't help but assent
Full of butterflies
More than I can vocalise

Lost

I feel I'm done
They have won
Gone is my backbone
I whinge and moan

Not even sure if there's a sun
I want to run
I thought I'd grown
Now it's thrown

There is no fun
I don't have anyone
Cold as stone
I am alone

Surprised

Thinking what is your deal?
What do you conceal?
Waiting for the lies
You'll be gone by sunrise

Round and round the same old wheel
Or could it be my heart you steal
I don't want to romanticise
Bet What if I have won the prize

Don't know what to feel
Could this be real
You aren't like other guys
You've really been the best surprise

Helpless

Do you call that alive?
Will you ever thrive?
I don't want to offend
That's not what I intend

Do you have drive?
Do you want to strive?
Your honor I can't defend
Your word i can't depend

I won't deprive
You won't arrive
You condescend
There is no end

Admiration

Someone who can advise
Someone to rationalise
Someone who sees I'm bright
Someone with foresight

Someone who will prioritise
Someone who can normalise
Someone who will not fight
Someone who will not spite

Someone who is wise
Someone to Idolise
Someone with insight
Someone who's always right

Sadness

I am defeated
I am depleted
I am broken
I have awoken

I've been cheated
It getting heated
Begins smoking
My life is token

Can I be deleted?
History repeated
Life has loudly spoken
Surely it is joking

Love

Our first moment is far from distinct
Love at first sight we are deprived of
Love in my life is surely extinct
Something I am unworthy of

My heart skipped, my life blinked
I preyed to the people up above
In that moment our souls linked
Could this really be true love?

So used to being hoodwinked
However, you fit me like a glove
I was sure it would be sussinct
Wrong. Now I know this is love.

Free

The freedom makes me want to dance
History behind me without a second glance
For I truely thought I'd see no end
That is how my life I would spend

Now a second chance
A new lease of life, a new stance
No need to bend
No need to lend

There's been a change of circumstance
Moving forward to advance
Watch me now as I attend
I smile and I commend

www.ingramcontent.com/pod-product-compliance
Lightning Source LLC
LaVergne TN
LVHW021348200726

843509LV00014B/2729